"An outer planet, a living moon perhaps." C.McC

Photographs by Jo Daniell

Introduction by Colleen McCullough

Text by Catherine Marshall

Thorn Bird Country

 WARNER BOOKS

A Warner Communications Company

Published by arrangement with Thames and Hudson Ltd, 30-34 Bloomsbury
Street, London WC1B 3QP, England

Warner Books, Inc., 75 Rockefeller Plaza, New York, N.Y. 10019

Ⓦ A Warner Communications Company

Printed in Japan

First United States printing: March 1983
10 9 8 7 6 5 4 3 2 1

Library of Congress Cataloging in Publication Data

Daniell, Jo.
   Thorn bird country.

   1. Australia—Description and travel—1981–
2. Marshall, Catherine, 1941–   . 3. Daniell, Jo.
I. Marshall, Catherine, 1941–   . II. Title.
DU105.2.D36 1983   919.4′0463   82-40394
ISBN 0-446-37573-X

(preceding pages)

1 Lake Mungo Station, western New South Wales

2 The Walls of China, Lake Mungo Station, western New South Wales

3, 4 The Walls of China, Lake Mungo Station, western New South Wales

5 Burke and Wills' last bedroom, Maidens Hotel

(on the Darling River), New South Wales

6 Maidens Hotel, Menindee, New South Wales

7 Shearer. Lake Mungo Station, western New South Wales

Introduction

Colleen McCullough

It is a hard country, even today. Times change, but the Australian heartland never does; despite all his tools and late twentieth-century aids, Man has scarcely scratched its surface.

Most of it lies as it has for countless millennia, sunk in a coma of ancient waterlessness. Millions of years have passed since it supported vast herds of animals at graze, if it ever did – though old-timers can remember days when kangaroos in their tens of thousands streamed leaping across the harsh hills. And I am old enough to remember kangaroos in thousands.

But the general impression is of an indifference to life, especially walking life. The birds are better equipped to reach infrequent water, and demand less of it; so too insects. As for plants, they have come to an understanding with the land by making all the concessions.

Color, and the quality of the light. An atmosphere either utterly invisible, or pulsating with haze and alluring blue mirages, or stuffed with dust thrown up by the long footsteps of the wind. A still whistling just beyond the human ear, a rhythmic boom-boom-boom of sheer heat, a huge sighing of leaf-blades, the rending bellow of thunder. Dust has a smell, appealing to the tuned nose, and after the first few minutes of a patiently awaited rain it gives forth the most exquisite perfume on this earth. Life in death smells not at all except at closest quarters, for there is too much air. The flowers in sheets mile upon mile sprung up after a winter shower mostly do not smell. Just the dust, and the sweetish ozone of a violent storm to remind one that the air is itself an entity.

To the eyes alone is offered a feast, and then only to those eyes which hunger after that particular kind of vision. Not everyone's vision by any means. Some eyes find it appalling, some depressing, some ugly, some too alien for love or liking while admitting to admiration. But for the hungry eyes, to rest upon the Australian heartland is literally a coming-home, a renewing of a self probably forged by it. Though some eyes love it instinctively in seeing it for the first time.

Introduction

I like to take photographs, and for the sort of amateur who understands the basics but harbors no pretension to a battery of different lenses, filters and cameras, I fancy I take quite a good photograph. Almost inevitably as I leaf through the many books of Australian pictures to be found particularly in Australian bookshops I find myself thinking, "Huh! My own photograph of X or Y is every bit as good as this professional one!" Probably too strict a judgment, for such things as the quality of printing and reproduction affect any photographer's work. However, I do stoutly maintain that most books of the Australian scene contain pictorial matter of no great distinction and certainly no great individuality.

Several years ago one of the editors at my publishers offered to show me some photographs of Australia's interior. And from the moment I set eyes upon the first one in a large series, I was a Jo Daniell admirer. As I said then, this man is the first photographer of my experience with the technical skill, the love, the understanding, and the soul to dig beneath the optical surface of Australia and show to eyes not there that truly Australia is a land so old it has become bald, wrinkled, desiccated, intractable, intolerant and incapable of looking any older. Time has ceased to tick for it, and his photographs reveal this.

They reveal much more, of course; they are works of art, a lenticular expansion of the eye inside the man's brain which sees more and comprehends more than his two eyes rigged only to perceive three-dimensional images. Vision is a most complex and tortuously evolved activity, dependent as much upon non-visual areas of the brain as upon the actual images transmitted by the eyes.

And that is where photographers usually fail. They point their cameras at an object their eyes see and allow their cameras no opportunity to depict more. So what appears on paper is something diminished rather than enhanced, for if it is a sweeping vista it is reduced to the size of a page instead of filling the

Introduction

gaze entirely, and if it is some tiny mite of a thing oozing a fluff of pollen its miniature beauty is lost by the size of the page.

Great photographs suggest more than the eye can see; they create a mood, they infect the imagination, they trigger emotions. And the viewer is left with permanent impressions far beyond mere sight; he becomes a part of the photographer's world, and understands those unseen parameters which give vision its profoundest impact.

I first looked at the photographs of Jo Daniell in an office through whose windows the crystalline explosion of Manhattan's glass towers stretched into the farthest distance. But there before my hungry eyes was a world I knew much better, to which my heart belonged. And yet in some ways I saw that world differently than I remembered it, so great was the photographer's art. The saurian eye in a ghost gum knot, looking out of a creamy integument with intelligence and a drowned, sad contemplation. Rank weeds sticking out of a field of snow in patent heat – but the snow was really salt. A stunning vulva in pink and grey rock. The odd square mirror of a spring leaping out of the shadows. What looked like the spent foam of a surfing beach was in reality the salt-encrusted bed of a dry creek. A tumbling red waterfall of rock. Mulga twigs dancing with the abandon of corybantes. New impressions of that most beautiful of all trees, the ghost gum.

I saw too how totally the land has rejected Man and how well it has succeeded in doing what few lands can do – make it impossible for Man to add his own brand of beauty. There, Man's scant imprints are downright ugly, his ability to create gorgeous gardens of delight thwarted. Nothing of his making belongs. The fences stutter away like stitches in a suppurating wound. The roads are earthen tracks fissured and convoluted by the runoff of rain. The buildings are shocks. The impedimenta cluttering these dwelling places are crude, dilapidated, *awful*. Even where Man has succeeded in tapping water from below, there blooms no oasis; the reluctant water seems slimy, the

Introduction

external signs of it are stark, primitive and totemistic. If the man-element in this collection of pictures reveals anything, it is that Man gave up, that he comes and goes across the land as a nomad and a thief. And that the land cares nothing for him, not love nor hate, not so much as a transient spasm of excusable disgust.

Ah, but the land itself! There are only four moods. Cloudless, overcast, high noon, beginning or end of day. The magical changes rung by the sovereign sun. My most cherished personal memory of the Australian heartland is of cloudless high noon, a deep red dune contoured against a cobalt sky, and like spears a few tussocks of brilliant green plant matter; a natural war between the elements, so crammed with color and contrast that I have never forgotten, never ceased to wonder. See the same country under a vault of clouds and it is an outer planet, a living moon perhaps, bleak and sere and bled of all vividness. And when the sun is low in the sky, thin lustrous blue shadows infiltrate between impossible yellows and oranges, the light on the rocks is purple, and the remote mountains are dark.

There is a danger in verbal rhapsody, that if overdone the reaction of the reader will end in antipathy. And I don't want to destroy the impact of these marvellous glimpses of a world I myself know and love.

The photography of Jo Daniell has to be regarded in two different ways. The first, as one highly sensitive man's portrayal of an alien and daunting country. The second, as the only significant photographic contribution to that very strong school of Australian art which has immortalized the Outback.

It is not customary to incorporate photographers among the ranks of artists, for the brush comes from the brain and transforms the external world into something intensely personal and individual. But occasionally a man with a camera has the genius to do just this; he can paint with a lens. Jo Daniell is primarily an artist. I commend him to you as such.

Commentary

CATHERINE MARSHALL

THIS BOOK IS THE RESULT of a journey undertaken by the photographer and writer during the winter of 1977. Our plan was to collect enough material to form a book on outback Australia, based on a selection of the best photographs and including an explanatory text.

Jo Daniell spent several months planning the trip, gathering information on the desert areas and organizing equipment and supplies. During this time, he realized that the challenge was far greater than he had at first thought. Over a period of three months he hoped to visit the five main deserts of central and western Australia – the Simpson, the Great Victoria, the Gibson, the Great Sandy and the Tanami. As it turned out the Tanami and the Great Victoria were too far to the north and south respectively to reach in the limited time available to us. However, we were prepared to let the country itself dictate our route.

The iconography of the central Australian wilderness is both graphic and vivid – bleached bones of drought-stricken animals, the tracery of mulga branches against sand dunes so red they seem vast rounded embers, the outlines of birds of prey against an intensely blue sky. Such country does not invite involvement. Most Australians, huddled on the coast in red-roofed cities, see it only in photographs.

The greatest challenge in photographing such country is to avoid the stereotyped images associated with it and to present a personal view which nevertheless captures the spirit of the landscape. The same problems exist when writing about it. The emphasis in this collaboration is on presenting our personal impressions of the country, both where they agree and where they differ.

We were somewhat limited by the necessary restrictions on photographing sacred sites and cave paintings of the aboriginals. In the past their trust in people professing to understand the intricacies of their cultural beliefs has been so often betrayed that few sites now remain unviolated. It has become crucial to preserve the sanctity of these sites in order to preserve an important part of aboriginal culture. Sadly, the significance of such places is now too often reduced to a few lines in an anthropological textbook instead of providing continuity to the beliefs of a tribe. Sacred sites are no longer tended, sacred song ceremonies lost to the desert air and ancient rituals forgotten. The old ways are fast disappearing. Too late we recognize that to photograph sacred paintings and objects is to desecrate them and bring anguish and grief to the tribe which created and preserved them.

The restrictions on photographing aboriginals whom we encountered on the trip were largely self-imposed. We had originally hoped, with naive optimism, to include photographs of tribal aboriginals, since to us the land and its people are inextricably linked. I had enjoyed as a child many aboriginal myths and legends and to me their Dreamtime spirits permeate every feature of the landscape. To show their way of life and their affinity with the land seemed to me essential to the book. As the journey progressed, however, we were forced to abandon this plan and look for a new approach.

The land of the aboriginal is infinitely expressive. He sees meaning in each rock, each tree, each waterhole, and seeks to preserve and protect it as its spirit protects him and his tribe. The question of aboriginal land rights is one of the most urgent confronting Australians. Too much tribal land has already been polluted, sacred sites desecrated and tribal groups displaced. With appalling arrogance and callousness white men have subjugated black men in Australia, forcing them to abandon ancient traditions and beliefs fundamental to their physical and spiritual well-being.

So those aboriginals we saw, trapped as they are between two societies, alienated from their tribal land, symbolized to us their dying culture. Their children and grandchildren will probably in time be absorbed and assimilated into white society. They may not miss the old ways, but as we travelled through their land seeing evidence of their destruction, we suffered a sad sense of loss for the cultural background we never had.

We returned from the trip acutely aware of what we had missed – a dry creek bed we'd have liked to follow, a rocky outcrop left unexplored, a tempting range of hills lying low on the horizon – but full of the joy of what we had discovered. The remoteness of the area intensified our feelings about it, instilling in us that vague sense of ownership felt towards secret places.

Our route had taken us into all the Australian States and the Northern Territory, from temperatures below freezing to over 30°C. In three months impressions crowded our minds to be enjoyed later at leisure. Since our return Jo's photographs have been exhibited successfully both here in Australia and overseas. Together with the text they form a selective record of an uncontained, intractable land – a wilderness to most of us. But to some it remains a cherished heritage, however far from it they find themselves, as long as their Dreamtime spirits remain.

"Civilized" Country

8 Drowned gum. Darling River, near Menindee, western New South Wales

10 Silverton, near Broken Hill, western New South Wales

9 Silverton, western New South Wales

"*New impressions of ghost gums.*" C.McC

12 Mulga Valley Station (deserted), western New South Wales

"*The buildings are shocks.*" C.McC

13 Child's bedroom. Mulga Valley Station (deserted)

11 Red river gums, Silverton, western New South Wales

14 Blacksmith's, Mulga Valley Station (deserted)

"The impedimenta of these dwelling places." C.McC

15 Mulga Valley Station (deserted)

16 (*overleaf*) Windmill at Mulyungarie Station,
western New South Wales

1 The Edge of Wilderness

In the silent lands
time broadens into space.
Approaching Port Augusta, going on,
iron-brown and limitless, the plains
were before me all day. Burnt mountains
fell behind
in the glittering sky.

LES MURRAY "The Wilderness"

WE LEFT MELBOURNE on June 22nd. The desert was our destination, the climax of our trip. Remoteness from civilization was the goal which inspired us, pushed us on through settled country into landscapes less defined by man's presence. As the pale yellow, empty areas on the maps we studied each night gradually expanded, our anticipation increased. The lack of detail excited us and held promise of unexpected discoveries.

Our first night was spent across the border in New South Wales. Victoria is a small state, closely settled and with widely varying terrain. Its northern boundary is the Murray River and across it lies the much larger state of New South Wales. Here the land broadens to extensive plains covered with saltbush and mallee scrub – famous sheep-grazing country.

We were still in settled areas and passing through farmlands, but crossing the Murray River at Swan Hill that evening we felt even then an exhilarating sense of freedom. We were on our way.

Our vehicle was a four-wheel-drive Toyota Landcruiser, loaded with empty petrol drums and several large water containers not yet needed but ready to be filled before we reached the desert areas. To be stranded in the desert without water means certain death within a few hours, so we tested our containers carefully before we left.

Petrol and water formed the bulk of our load, together with spare tyres, a large box of spare parts, a minimum of personal gear, food – of Jo's choosing – and half a dozen casks of wine, also chosen by Jo. Enough to last the journey as I rarely drink alcohol and had decided the trip offered a good opportunity to go on a diet.

We were equipped with a two-way radio, essential for the areas we planned to visit, and an extra car battery for the occasional luxury of playing tapes on the cassette deck. On top of the vehicle were several rolls of carpet which Jo was to photograph in outback settings for an advertising campaign, an extra job to help finance the trip. These were to weigh us down a lot and prove troublesome until we were able to offload them, but the delays they caused were minor. In general we felt we were well prepared and ready to go.

Key to photographs

Ayers Rock 26, 27, 29–31
Bedourie 69, 70
Coober Pedy 20, 21
Cordillo Downs 72, 74, 75
Darling River 5, 8
Flinders Ranges 80, 82
Gibson Desert 38, 63–65
Great Sandy Desert 51–55, 59, 61, 62, 67
Killagurra Spring 56
Kondoolka Station 17–19
Lake Blanche 81
Lake Disappointment 57, 58, 60
Lake Everard 23, 24
Lake Harris 25
Lake Mungo Station 1–4, 7
Macdonnell Ranges 66
Meekatharra 49
Menindee 6
Mount Lyndhurst Station 78, 79
Mulga Valley Station 12–15
Mulyungarie Station 16
Musgrave Ranges 28
New South Wales 1–16
Northern Territory 26, 27, 29–36, 68
Olgas, The 32–36
Queensland 71
Silverton 9–11
South Australia 17–25, 28, 72–82
Sturt's Stony Desert 72–77
Welbourn Hill 22
Western Australia 37–55, 61–65
Wiluna 47, 48

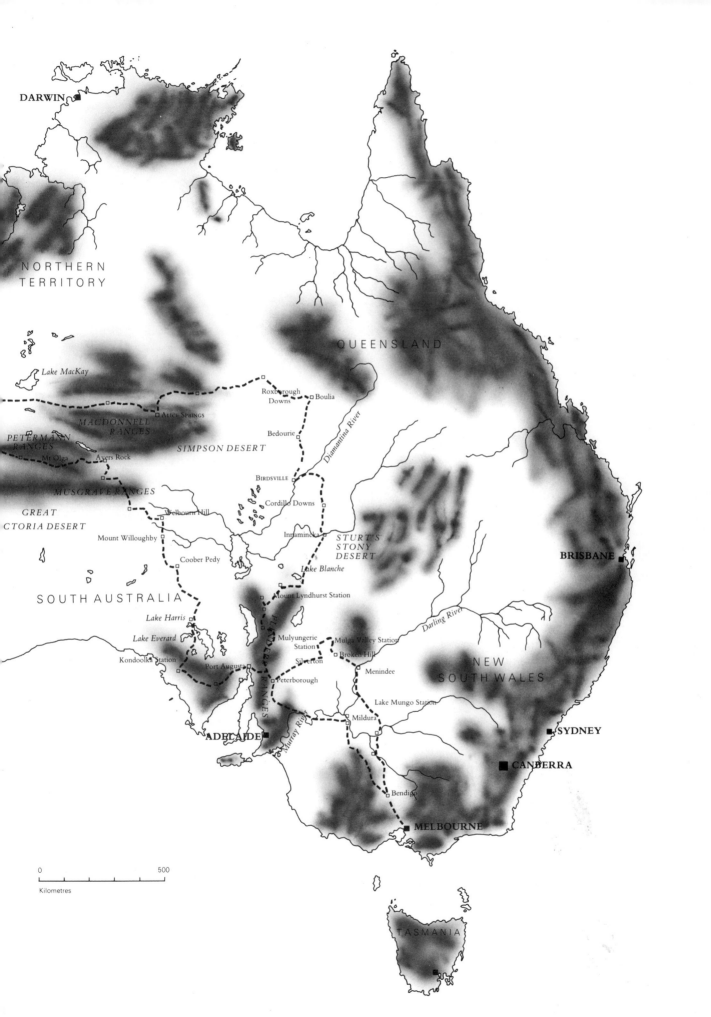

DARWIN

NORTHERN
TERRITORY

QUEENSLAND

Lake MacKay

Roxborough
Downs   Boulia

MACDONNELL
RANGES   Alice Springs

PETERMANN   Bedourie
RANGES   SIMPSON DESERT

Mr Olga   Ayers Rock

MUSGRAVE RANGES   BIRDSVILLE

GREAT   Welbourn Hill   Cordillo Downs
VICTORIA DESERT

Mount Willoughby   Innamincka   STURT'S
                                                      STONY
                    Coober Pedy   Lake Blanche   DESERT

SOUTH AUSTRALIA   BRISBANE

Lake Harris   Mount Lyndhurst Station

Lake Everard   Darling River
                        Mulyungerie   Mulga Valley Station
Kondoolka Station   Station   NEW
                        Silverton   Broken Hill   SOUTH WALES
        Port Augusta
                        Peterborough   Menindee

                                          Lake Mungo Station   SYDNEY

ADELAIDE   Mildura   CANBERRA
                    Murray River

                                    Bendigo

                                    MELBOURNE

0   500

Kilometres

TASMANIA

The weather was cold, mid-winter in the southern states, and often at night the temperature dropped below freezing. We had brought a tent, but used it only when there was a wind or rain, preferring to withdraw from the landscape as little as possible. Walls of orange nylon removed this close contact and deprived us of an immediate awareness of our surroundings when we woke in the morning. Despite the rewards of this stoical attitude we suffered nights of little sleep spent rekindling a dying fire over which to huddle until morning light. An attitude perversely ignoring the sensible advice of all camping manuals.

After crossing the Murrumbidgee River at Balranald we headed north-west along rough station tracks towards Lake Mungo, an area which has become famous as the site of Australia's oldest archaeological discoveries. We approached it with the knowledge that this vast, windswept, sandy plain rimmed with eroded dunes was once a fertile environment which supported in abundance large populations of aboriginals over thousands of years. Though not a great distance from the closely settled areas bordering the Murray River, this region of the outback seemed, on a grey, overcast day, to be as remote and desolate as any we would see.

Australia is the most ancient land mass on earth. No great geological upheavals have occurred in this continent since before the Permian Period, 200 million years ago, when earth movements thrust upwards the highest mountains to form a range extending almost the length of the eastern coastline. Since then, activity has decreased, the land has stirred slightly, grumbled occasionally and then settled to long eras of relative stability, while elsewhere in the world cataclysms changed the face of continents.

Before the Lake Mungo discoveries it was thought that man had not inhabited Australia until comparatively recent times. Even the assessment formed after the first find has since been revised several times as fresh discoveries were made. Now evidence of Homo sapiens (modern man) unearthed at Lake Mungo dates human occupation there back 38,000 years, and the area still has much to yield.

We drove along a rough track made muddy by a recent fall of rain and eventually stood on the north-eastern shore of the dry lake bed, a rim of eroded sand dunes 12 miles long known as The Walls of China. Ahead of us lay a desolate plain covered with saltbush, a dull grey-green colour under an overcast sky, the only sound the moaning of the strong wind constantly carving the bizarre pale yellow sand sculptures on which we stood.

The term "lake" in outback Australia is misleading. More often than not it indicates the past rather than the present condition of a network of creeks and billabongs long dried up. Very rarely a severe flood will fill within hours ancient water courses and crusted lake beds where the only surface movement for decades has been shifting sands. When this happens, the surrounding desert is transformed for a brief season into a profusion of brilliantly coloured wildflowers and plants, a display so vivid as almost to deny the dormant, subtle years preceding it.

Lake Mungo is older than most. Once part of an ancient water system flowing through south-western New South Wales, it has been dry for 16,000 years. The landscape in that far-off time when nomads camped on its shores was vastly different from what it is today. When full, the lake sustained a wide area of lush vegetation and a variety of wildlife. The nomads lived well on plentiful supplies of fish and freshwater mussels from the lake, emu eggs and game which they hunted in the surrounding scrub.

Before the sand yielded its secrets, all clues to their way of life lay buried beneath the dunes bordering the waterless lake. These dunes, etched into myriad still-born rivulets and weird jutting small-scale mountains, have become a tourist attraction as well as an area of archaeological study. The erosion has helped to unearth valuable finds which encourage scientists to mount subsequent excavations. In 1968 human bones were uncovered by erosion at the southern end of the dunes and these provided evidence not only of their antiquity but of the surprising complexity of aboriginal culture so long ago.

A young aboriginal woman had been ritually cremated, the bones broken and again burnt, and the remains buried in a shallow hole in the sand. Radio-carbon dating tests on the bones indicated that the ceremony had taken place over 25,000 years ago, the oldest evidence in the world of a ritual cremation. Other discoveries dated back a further 12,000 years – charcoal from ancient fireplaces, debris from meals, stone tools, all providing clues to the way of life of the early nomads.

Now the shifting dunes have taken over where once tall eucalyptus offered shade. In this bleak landscape it was hard to imagine a refuge for any living creature. A paradoxical outback, whose apparent timelessness is time concealed, history hidden.

I went walking while Jo took photographs, and focused down from the overall impression of undisturbed yellowness to find to my surprise evidence of great activity. Comings and goings of a variety of creatures: kangaroo tracks and emu tracks were instantly recognizable, the tracks of small nocturnal marsupials and lizards less so, despite our portable collection of books on flora and fauna to which we constantly referred. Nevertheless, the evidence of such traffic softened the landscape, relieved the harshness of the environment so that I left Lake Mungo feeling that not all life had drained from it with its water.

On the way back we stopped at Mungo Station, one of two sheep stations now occupying the former lake. These once formed part of a vast half-million acre station, Gol Gol, which was subdivided into 40,000-acre properties after the First World War. The main shearing-shed for Gol Gol, built of Murray pine 110 years ago by Chinese labourers employed on the station, now stands on Mungo and is itself a tourist attraction. We were lucky enough to arrive there during the shearing season and see it in use. The atmosphere, the smells, the sounds of an Australian shearing shed are unique, and in this one, mellowed with age and use, the wool press piled high with creamy fleece, it was easy to imagine its heyday. The shed then had thirty blade-shearers and later was converted to eighteen machine stands. Now only four remain, but the past hangs in the air with the heady smell of greasy wool.

Friday, June 24.

8 p.m. Camped out from Mungo Station towards Pooncarrie. Set up camp and enjoyed an enormous steak and a glass of wine. I didn't realize I'd be so hungry. So much for the diet.

Drove all morning through marvellous saltbush plains. Saw several mobs of kangaroos – greys and magnificent reds – some grazing by side of track. We sat quietly as they scratched themselves, watching us, ears twitching.

Mobs of emus along the track, running swiftly and stupidly with no sense of direction. Watched absorbed as two pairs of wedge-tailed eagles soared in slow motion high above us. Glorious flight – so free. Disturbed one about to swoop on a small bird. It's a joy to see our wildlife free in the environment and not in a zoo. They belong to the plains.

I'm finding the scrubland always interesting, never boring, never the dreary, monotonous waste it appears to so many. The colours vary from washed-out greens to subdued reds and browns, always so subtle. Here you're forced to look beyond the first impression, to observe detail, to train your eyes to pick out the soft grey kangaroos from the landscape and the grey-brown emus from the surrounding scrub. The rich beauty of European forests seems too obvious after this, too easily appreciated. And yet this is a much older landscape, worn down by time, passive and long-suffering, enduring the severest droughts, heaviest floods and devastating winds. Its vegetation bends, distorts, adapts – and survives.

Saturday, June 25.

4.30 a.m. Very cold night. Started off mild and it seemed good enough to sleep out, but a heavy frost formed towards morning and we nearly froze. Jo's sleeping bag became sodden and he got up at 4 a.m. and lit a fire to dry off. I hardly slept at all despite a sweater over my track suit and 2 pairs of socks, so I got dressed and huddled over the fire. The blaze is comforting. We lit the Primus lamp for more light and I'm writing this beside it.

I really should have brought an extra blanket but I thought the sleeping bag would be warm enough – I think I'll get a cheap one today if we reach Menindee before 12.

The settlement of Australia by Europeans extends back only to the end of the 18th century, not a long period compared to America and other earlier colonies. For many years the colony's growth was limited by the difficulties of exploring unknown territory to the west, so that much pastoral country in the outback was opened up to settlers little more than 120 years ago.

Menindee on the Darling River was one of the early outposts established as a depot for the makeshift sheep- and cattle-runs of the north. The area west of the Darling was still largely unknown to all but a few hardy pioneers in search of new grazing lands, and the extreme heat, scarcity of waterholes and aboriginal tribes hostile to the takeover of their land inhibited further expansion.

The way of life was rough and the isolation intense, at times overpowering. Bullock teams came in once a year from Melbourne with basic supplies of a crude kind – "flour (with or without weevils), poor quality 'post and rail' tea (containing many stalks which floated to the top of the brew), dark brown ration sugar and plug tobacco, black and pungent." The wagons returned laden with bales of wool from the surrounding stations.

My grandfather, who was a drover and later a hawker in the district towards the end of the century, often described to my father the many colourful characters who passed through the Darling outposts on their way to work on the station. Long months of isolation and hardship accentuated peculiarities of temperament and bred the sort of eccentricity which belongs to the past, enriching the pioneer communities.

It was under such extreme conditions that the Australian concept of "mateship" was born, that bond beyond friendship between fellow sufferers. Despite the hardship and deprivation of the times, the austere way of life possessed epic qualities rare today. Men who walked for weeks in above-century temperatures for work on outback stations were a regular sight. Time in which to achieve such efforts was the reward of the age.

Menindee today is still very much an outback town, whose dusty streets and buildings recall its early history. It was here that the explorers Burke and Wills established a base camp before attempting to cross the unknown centre of Australia to reach its northern shores. The story of their epic journey demonstrates the mystique which surrounded explorers of the Victorian era, most of them eager amateurs with little in common but supreme self-confidence and a sense of adventure. Caution and forethought were often sacrificed to a desire to be first to open new territory. So it was with the Burke and Wills expedition.

In 1860 the South Australian and Victorian governments each offered a bounty to the first expedition to cross Australia from south to north. The challenge increased the already existing rivalry between the colonies and lent an atmosphere of haste to the preparations. The Victorian expedition was the most costly ever to attack the Australian wilderness. Led by Robert O'Hara Burke, a former superintendent of police at Castlemaine, it was financed by the Royal Society of Victoria and overequipped from the start. On August 20, 1860, the party of 17 men, 27 camels, 22 horses and a collection of heavily loaded wagons was farewelled from Melbourne by a crowd of thousands.

Even before they had left the settled areas east of the Darling, quarrels broke out and the party was divided. Several wagons broke down under excessive loads and by the time they reached Menindee five men had either resigned or been dismissed. Burke was a volatile leader and, although brave, had no experience of the bush and its hazards.

In Menindee the arrival of the party and its impedimenta caused amazement and scepticism amongst the settlers. The last outpost before the Centre, Menindee then consisted of a few shacks, a shanty pub in which Burke and Wills slept, a store and a landing-stage for the river steamers.

Burke established a base camp some miles up the Darling, where he decided to leave the bulk of the expedition and lead a small advance party on to Cooper's Creek more than 400 miles to the north. The rear group was to follow with the heavy stores and rejoin Burke's party at Cooper's Creek before the next stage of the journey was attempted. On the way to Cooper's Creek, Burke sent William Wright back to Menindee to organize and lead the rear group. He chose wrongly, and this as well as a series of mishaps caused Wright to delay for more than three months before following the advance party. He was never to rejoin it.

Burke made camp on Cooper's Creek and there, under conditions of extreme heat and discomfort, waited impatiently for Wright's party to arrive. After more than a month he decided to "dash into the interior and cross the continent at all hazards." He again split his party into two groups, one group under the charge of William Brahe to remain at Cooper's Creek depot until Burke returned, and the other, consisting of himself, William Wills, John King and Charlie Gray, to head north towards the Gulf of Carpentaria. They took with them six camels, one horse and enough supplies for three months, on the understanding that if they had not returned within that time Brahe was to head back to Menindee. Burke was anxious to take advantage of the full waterholes promised by recent falls of rain and was confident of reaching the Gulf and returning to Cooper's Creek well within the three-month limit.

The four men set off in good spirits. Ahead of them lay a journey of 1,500 miles to the Gulf and back, mostly on foot, since the animals were needed to carry water and stores. It was the wrong time of year to travel in the tropics – the wet season, steamy, muddy, subject to frequent tremendous downpours of rain, excessively hot by day and night. They reached the wide marshlands of the northern shores on February 11, 1861, eight weeks after leaving the depot on Cooper's Creek. They had four weeks' supplies left for the return journey.

Sickness slowed them down considerably. Burke suffered dysentery and Gray could hardly walk. Food soon ran short and they were forced to kill some of the camels and the horse and eat their meat. Lack of fresh fruit and vegetables almost certainly resulted in the party's contracting scurvy. Had they known of native plants other than nardoo, their condition might have been alleviated, but they retained to the end that peculiar unwillingness and inability to adapt to an alien environment, to adopt the ways of the bush.

Gray was the first to die. On April 21, Burke, Wills and King reached the depot at Cooper's Creek to find a message from Brahe stating that his party had left camp only seven hours before, after waiting four months for Burke's return. This tragic mischance destroyed any hopes they had of gaining the strength needed to return to Melbourne. They decided to head in a south-west direction along the creek towards the nearest settlement 150 miles away, but the attempt proved hopeless.

Considerably weakened by malnutrition, Wills remained behind in a makeshift hut while Burke and King went in search of aboriginals, now their only hope of survival. He died there shortly after they left. Burke died a day or two later. King was taken in by aboriginals who cared for him until a search party found him two months later.

So ended the Burke and Wills expedition. What might have been an epic of survival in the outback is now a famous part of Australian history as a tragedy of errors and mismanagement.

We visited the room in the pub where Burke and Wills slept when they reached Menindee, saw other evidence of their stay there, felt their presence on the banks of the Darling where they set up camp. And, a century later, mourned them.

Silverton is an entirely different outback town from Menindee. A ghost town, a relic of the mining boom which drew men to the far west of New South Wales during the 1880s, it lies in beautiful country 15 miles north-west of Broken Hill. Originally called Umberumberka ("native rat-hole") it was renamed for the rich silver deposits found nearby in the Barrier Ranges. It quickly grew from a tent-and-shanty settlement of 250 inhabitants in 1883 to a thriving town of 3,000 in 1885–86, and just as quickly declined. The small pockets of high-grade ore had become exhausted, and the miners and their families departed for the newly discovered Broken Hill mining field. Now less than 100 people live in the town.

The atmosphere belongs to the past although only traces remain of streets once thronged with miners and horses and wagons, their outlines marked by occasional crumbling ruins and dilapidated buildings. Best of these were the remaining miners' cottages of stone, recalling the rigorous way of life endured for the chance of making a fortune. A transitory town, with such a very brief period between development and decline – perhaps only a day – that the anticipation of a strike still hangs in the air, as if a camera flashed once in the past and caught the feeling for ever.

From Silverton we took station tracks towards the South Australian border, heading in a roundabout way for Port Augusta where we planned to stock up on petrol and supplies. The most spectacular sight of the day came when we topped a rise and saw Mundi Mundi Plain at dusk – saltbush flatness as far as the eye could see, washed with the soft dying colours of the sun and contained only by a pure, slightly curved horizon, truly the perimeter of the earth.

Monday, June 27.

Camped last night in dry creek bed. Beautiful country from Broken Hill – red soil, superb river red gums along dry creek beds. These trees, the pale sturdiness of their thick twisted trunks, are immensely moving, the survivors of drought and flood. We made a fire from the debris collected around their trunks in times of flood – leaves, bark, branches, the broken skeletons of trees less able to withstand the rushing water.

Left campsite before 8 following rough dirt tracks through remote properties. Saw very large flock of white cockatoos – Little Corellas – screeching wildly on a dry dam at Wilangee Station.

Turned off in direction of border along an overgrown track which led us to an abandoned property – an illusion of civilization.

"Mulga Valley," an old corrugated iron homestead and outbuildings, had been deserted long ago and left to crumble into the red soil. Completely isolated, surrounded by mulga saltbush plains gradually reclaiming the remains of a garden. No sound but a biting wind – an eerie quality to the place.

A door was open and we wandered through, careful not to disturb anything. We felt intruders in another era, entering rooms scarcely disturbed for decades. In the dining room, antique furniture, a dresser full of delicately embroidered tablecloths and napkins, china displayed in a china cabinet. In a bedroom an old iron cot beside a cedar chest of drawers, at the window light filtering through tattered remnants of beautiful lace curtains. A wood stove in the kitchen with wood nearby, pots and pans no longer used, the crackle and clatter and clamour stilled into an unnatural silence. Rooms of memories, haunting and poignant, the dusty greyness of neglect obscuring their colour and detail.

Elsewhere, surrounding the house, an atmosphere of decay. Rusted machinery, broken-down sheds, an underground coolhouse crumbling into ruin. In one of the sheds we found an old red truck, rusted into stillness, the name painted proudly on the side: "N. G. Trusler, Mulga Valley via Silverton."

Behind the house were large shearers' quarters, evidently in use during the shearing season, so the property is still used for grazing sheep. But the impression which remained with us was one of civilization been and gone, of the bush reclaiming its own.

Mulga Valley represented the past, the early days of outback settlement. Over the next week we saw similar homesteads, abandoned and succumbing to the encroaching bush. Due to the indiscriminate clearance of land over the past century, desert areas are spreading and overwhelming formerly fertile land. Many families have been forced off the land to seek a living in the cities or in a less hostile environment and in some areas the population is less now than it was 50 years ago. Here outback settlement is less vigorous, even retrogressive, lacking the continuity of family ownership and involvement.

The costs of running a large station have increased so much that in the more remote areas properties owned and managed by the same family over generations are now rare. The larger properties are usually owned by companies and run by managers and the staff kept to a minimum.

It's difficult to imagine the loneliness and isolation of such a life. We formed some idea of it when we crossed the South Australian border and after a hard, tiring day's travel entered Mulyungarie Station.

Today was exhausting. From Mulga Valley we took a scarcely used track in a south-west direction across the plains. We had to take compass bearings along the way since the track constantly disappeared and what looked to be a visible track on Jo's army maps turned out to be no more than a cattle track.

We eventually struck the South Australian border – a dingo-proof fence – and had to travel miles in both directions from the point where we met it to find a gate to go through into South Australia. I had a hunch we should go north along it to strike the track we wanted and Jo wanted to follow the compass bearings. He turned out to be right – a lucky guess – but only after hours of travelling across the plains until finally we came into the station we were headed for, Mulyungarie, an immense outback property with a school for the children of the employees. The kids came out to meet us and directed us to the manager's house. By this time we were really tired and strained, and irritable, although considering the pressure on us to arrive at a property, any property, to see a sign of civilization, we got along very well by just remaining silent for most of the way.

The manager's wife welcomed us and made us a cup of coffee. She was evidently so lonely – had been there for twenty years – that people were a luxury she wanted to enjoy as long as possible. "It's the loneliness that's hardest to bear – gets you down sometimes. But I couldn't live in the city. I like coming back here." She pressed us to stay the night but we decided to move on to the Peterborough road and make up some time.

Once on the highway, we kept on for a couple of hours before we crossed country to camp. The highway was unremittingly flat with no trees visible on either side. When we found some it was completely dark and raining (it was a testing day for us!) and we ended up camped beside the railway. But we were too tired and cold to go on. There was a strong wind blowing and we had a terrible time getting the tent up, disagreeing about the best way to do it. At least the rain stopped, thank goodness, I got a good fire burning and we relaxed with steak, tomato and onion salad and some wine. A few minutes later the train passed about three feet away from where we sat, practically shattering our eardrums. We broke down laughing – what else? – and felt a lot better then. Also, I had two glasses of wine to cheer me up – I think I'm becoming an alcoholic. On top of everything, a bottle of oil I had leaked all through my clothes, so it's been one of those days.

But it's a beautiful clear night now and the stars are glorious. We've been listening to Paganini on the radio and we haven't had a train through for at least an hour.

I've never seen country so flat. The saltbush plains seem to go on for ever. But despite the deceptive monotony of the landscape we love travelling through it. It's tremendously exhilarating to be the only people in the world, and the country is so rich in wildlife. On Mulyungarie we saw the biggest mob of kangaroos either of us had ever seen, together with a mob of emus. They were so much a part of the background that the whole plain seemed to be moving right to the horizon, its hard line undulating and softened by their motion.

We've done over a thousand miles so far, and on our seventh day we're getting along well together and enjoying the trip.

Kondoolka, where we arrived several days later after stocking up on supplies at Port Augusta, was a sheep station of 600 square miles, a beautiful property owned by friends of Jo's. They were kind enough to let us use the homestead while they were away in Adelaide and we stayed several days.

Our first morning there, a clear cold morning, we drove with the manager through mallee and saltbush country to see aboriginal cave paintings at Wallaby Mountain. The huge outcroppings of rust-coloured granite formed many caves and hollows with some paintings discernible on the surfaces, not very clear after many years of neglect. In the past, aboriginal tribes regularly refurbished their sacred paintings in order to preserve their potency and significance. Now, sadly, the red and ochre earth colours they used have faded. I made out an emu and abstract symbolic drawings on ceilings and walls, probably well over 100 years old. One cave with animal tracks painted on the walls might have been a sacred hunting cave. We looked at maps of aboriginal tribal areas and saw it was Wilangu territory. Now all gone.

I felt their presence in the area more strongly than Jo did. I imagined them on the red plain below Wallaby Mountain, hunting kangaroos through the mallee scrub. Jo was always more conscious in places like Menindee of the presence of the early explorers such as Burke and Wills, so we reinforced each other's interest.

After we left Kondoolka we entered a desolate landscape varying from rich red soil with mulga and mallee scrub to grey-pink clay and silvery green saltbush. For the first time we felt we were really getting beyond all traces of civilization. In summer it would have been unbearable, but now it held the fascination of being potentially threatening, wild country.

We passed on the right of Lake Everard, a large salt lake pan, and drove across country to the edge of it, got under the dog fence and walked over it – a weird feeling like stepping on another planet. A range of new colours – yellow-grey basin edged with dark purple-coloured shrubs, some sort of flowering saltbush which we couldn't identify.

That night we camped near sand dunes bordering Lake Harris, on the way to Kingoonya. We had seen them from the track, our first sand dunes of the trip, and decided to head for them and camp the night. We drove for some distance across country and came upon them in the late afternoon light, glowing with the sun and marked with deep-set wind patterns. Huge and pure, they curved across the horizon. Yellow sand with clumps of shrubs scattered on them. We ran to the top of the nearest of them and saw more beyond. The wind blowing across the dunes was strong and biting cold, and our footprints deep in the sand were quickly filled in and obliterated.

Next morning we saw the salt lake in the early light – a wide white border of salt crystals heavily encrusted around the edge of a shallow pool of water, forming hardened ripples of salt. I tasted it and it was very salty and strong. We went walking on the lake bed near the water and the surface was hard and packed. The morning light caught the dunes and reflected them in the water. Together with the gleaming salt crystals, it was a strange and beautiful sight.

We were a long way behind schedule and anxious to reach the Aboriginal Reserve in the north-west corner of South Australia before heading into the Northern Territory and central Australia. We passed through Kingoonya and Coober Pedy as quickly as possible, stopping only for supplies and petrol.

Travelling had become uncomfortable. The road through Coober Pedy was heavily corrugated and red dust hung thickly in the air, getting into everything. We longed to escape the tourist traffic and the bleak towns which spoilt an otherwise pure environment. Coober Pedy, on a sun-baked stony plain, was the most depressing place imaginable. A town of opal miners and aboriginals, all so totally uprooted from their cultural backgrounds that the town seems crass, without continuity. We were glad to leave, and camped an hour out of town and a world away in a dry creek-bed lined with ghost gums.

Tuesday, July 5.

Stopped several times today for repairs to car. Coil gone – Jo is going to replace it tomorrow. Hot gibber plains – scarcely any vegetation except grass tussocks. Some mulga and eucalyptus along water courses. Passed through large stations – Mt. Willoughby, where we got petrol, and Welbourn Hill, which Jo photographed. Dust everywhere – we're covered in it all the time. Driving into huge afternoon sun – very hard to see ahead. Camped tonight past Marla Bore on way to Indulkana. I made damper tonight, which worked out reasonably well, thank goodness. This morning I dropped the bacon and eggs in the dust. Tomorrow we head for the Centre.

Dead Centre

17 (*preceding page*) Shearing shed, Kondoolka
Station, South Australia

18, *19* Mount Wallaby, Kondoolka Station,
South Australia

20 Sunset on the 9 Mile, Coober Pedy, South Australia

21 Itinerant foxshooters outside Coober Pedy

"*Man goes across the land like a nomad and a thief.*" C.McC

22 (*overleaf*) Welbourn Hill Station,
South Australia

23 Lake Everard (salt), South Australia

24 Dune at Lake Everard. *"So old it has become bald, wrinkled, desiccated . . ."* C.McC

25 Dunes at Lake Harris (salt), South Australia

26 Dawn at Uluru (Ayers Rock), Northern Territory

27 Dusk at Uluru

28 Hadrian's Wall, Musgrave Ranges, South Australia

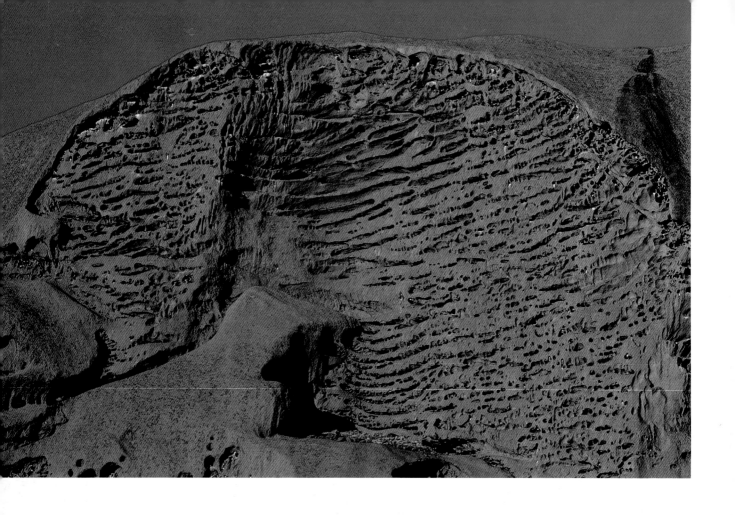

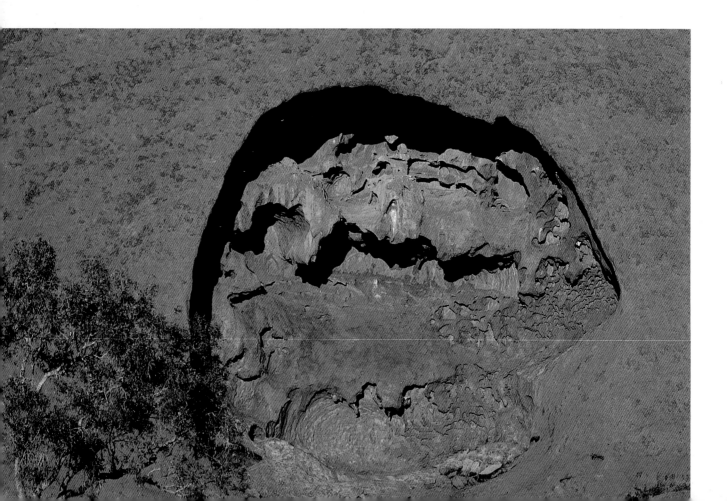

29, 30, 31 Ayers Rock, dusk at Uluru, Northern Territory

"*A tumbling red waterfall of rock.*" C.McC

32, 33 Katatjuta, at dawn and dusk (the Olgas), Northern Territory

34 Wildflowers at Katatjuta
"A tiny mite of a thing oozing a fluff of pollen". C.McC

35 Katatjuta (the Olgas) at dusk

36 Katatjuta (the Olgas) at dawn, Northern Territory

2 The Centre

We belong here, we are of the old ways.
We are the corroboree and the bora ground,
We are the old sacred ceremonies, the laws of the elders.
We are the wonder tales of Dream Time, the tribal legends told.
We are the past

KATH WALKER "We Are Going"

IN THE BEGINNING, the world was a flat, featureless plain. There was no life, no creatures, no trees, no plants, no hills or watercourses.

Then, long long ago, during the *Tjukurpa*, the Dreamtime, the Ancestors of all living creatures rose from the plain and wandered the earth. And where each of these great animal-like beings wandered, where he slept, made fire or dug for water, a natural feature was formed to mark his passage and the land was instilled eternally with his *Kurunpa*, his life essence. So was the world created and so it remains.

All men are directly descended from their totemic Ancestors and bound for life to the land created by them. Each feature of a man's tribal land, each tree, each rock, each waterhole along the route of the First Journey, contains the *Kurunpa* of his Ancestor. He sees recorded in the surrounding landscape the ancient story of his own beginning. Each time he travels through it he experiences the infinite joy of regeneration.

A man lives according to the unchanging laws of the Dreamtime, which is eternal and ever-present. 'As it was in the Beginning, is now, and ever shall be.' He is one with all living creatures with whom he shares a common beginning, no greater and no less a part of creation than the hare wallaby, the emu, the lizard, the snake which share his land. He dies and is no more, but the *Kurunpa* of his Ancestor remains forever in his land and in his people. And so it continues.

In the Dreamtime, Uluru rose miraculously out of a large flat sandhill. Ten different totemic Beings created its features, its caves, its waterholes, its crevices, and where they lived and died and fought each other, these places became sacred sites visited by the Pitjantjatjara and Yankuntjatjara people.

In 1873 Uluru was seen by a white man for the first time. The explorer W.C. Gosse described it as "the most wonderful natural feature I have ever seen" and named it Ayers Rock after the South Australian Premier. The following year the explorer Ernest Giles wrote of the rock, "Its appearance and outline is most imposing, for it is simply a mammoth monolith that rises out of the sandy desert soil around, and stands with a perpendicular and totally inaccessible face at all points, except one slope at the North-West end."

All descriptions fail to convey the awesome beauty of Uluru, its massive size, its majestic grandeur and its utter appropriateness to its setting. It rises cleanly and abruptly from the flat red plain, visible from half a day away, a bare rounded mountain ribbed with deep vertical grooves. The most ancient feature in this oldest of landscapes, it is now recognized as one of the most spectacular landforms in the world.

Uluru is composed of feldspar-rich sandstone called arkose, deposited in layers on the sea floor during the Cambrian Period over 500 million years ago. The sandstone layers were tipped on end during a period of violent earth movement, and these cause the vertical banding which is a prominent feature of the rock. Its massive form, likened to that of an "enormous pebble," is due to the relative absence of weaknesses or faults in the composition of the rock, so that it has maintained its unique shape over millions of years. Long-continued erosion of the softer rocks surrounding it lowered the land surface and formed the wide plain from which it now rises as the visible top of a huge partially-buried sandstone mass. Its present shape was probably formed about 40 million years ago when it rose as an island above a large lake.

In the last few million years the only changes to the rock have been superficial, the results of erosion. The most obvious effect of weathering is widespread flaking of the rock's surface, causing its characteristic smooth, rounded outline. Its rusty red coloring is due to the coating of iron oxides formed by the action of water and oxygen on iron in the minerals. This aggravates the flaking process by causing the minerals to expand, increasing the outward pressure on the crust so that it peels off in thin layers.

Water, wind and abrupt changes in temperature result in different weathering effects, seen in several beautiful cave formations and surface features. One of the most spectacular shapes gouged out of the surface of the rock by wind and rain is Ngoru, meaning ritual chest scars, an intricate pattern of grooves and hollows on the northern face. In the Dreamtime, this was the camp of the first Hare Wallaby men, the *Mala*, during their initiation ceremonies.

Today few aboriginals visit Uluru, once so sacred and beloved a place. Its secret crevices where wallabies feed, its painted caves, its precious waterholes have all been desecrated and their significance lost forever. To know this is to suffer within oneself a conflict of emotions, either to mourn the lost heritage of Uluru or to enjoy the geological marvel of Ayers Rock. To most, a conflict between imagination and reality. But invested as it is with the beliefs of the people whom it has sustained and nourished over thousands of years, its features infused with the spirits of their Ancestors, Uluru emanates power and majesty. Its sense of oneness, of unity, is truly religious. It fulfills its significance, it becomes what we make of it, however the means of its creation.

Friday, July 8.

Up at 6 this morning to catch early morning light on Ayers Rock. We reached it just as the sun rose to strike the eastern face, highlighting the ridges in its surface and casting deep shadows into the hollows and crevices. An awesome sight.

Arrived at the campsite before 9 and checked in with the ranger. We plan to spend the day exploring the rock, and getting clean, which could take a week. I'm absolutely filthy. We're both taking on rather simian characteristics, with hands like monkey paws. So we go around scratching and grunting at each other. I'm looking forward to a shower.

10 p.m. A good day. I feel clean and refreshed. I was able to do all the washing while Jo did maintenance work on the car.

The days are very warm now, but the nights still cold. We had lunch over the campfire and went driving around the rock. Those marvellous fissures and holes in the sandstone are full of incredible detail, but the colours of the rock leave the deepest impression – the rich red against the brilliant deep blue sky. A small animal was scratching in one of the cavities, the sound magnified within the hole. A number of dingoes around – we heard them howling this morning and again this evening. And when we were out driving this afternoon we saw a young dingo on the plain and tried to coax him over. Crows are everywhere – they picked open a whole box of tissues which we'd left out.

Tomorrow night we hope to camp at the Olgas.

Katatjuta, a cluster of domed mountains twenty miles to the west of Uluru, stands in isolation on the same flat plain, the second of central Australia's great natural features. Named Mt. Olga by the explorer Ernest Giles and known in group form as the Olgas, they rise from the plain as enormous round-topped pillars separated by steep narrow chasms to form a semicircle around an inner valley.

To many they are more spectacular than Uluru and are steeped in as rich a mythology. The pillars of the south-western corner are the metamorphosed bodies of the Kangaroo, the Euro (a hill kangaroo) and the Night Owl, whose activities in the area, as well as those of other Dreamtime Ancestors, determined the features of Katatjuta.

From a distance, Katatjuta is an impressive sight, its domes appearing like huge boulders resting on the horizon. In the evening light they glowed purple and blue against the deepening orange sky, ever-changing as we approached them, gradually assuming their individual shapes and detail.

We camped not far from them just as darkness fell, and positioned ourselves so that we would wake with them immediately in view. They were even more impressive in the morning light. Like Uluru, they are a rich red colour, smooth and rounded, but composed of a coarse conglomerate made up of boulders and pebbles cemented together by fine sandstone. They were raised as mountains during the Cambrian Period and eroded down to their present dome shape over a period of 500 million years. The deep narrow valleys between them are the result of erosion on zones of weakness in the original rock mass.

Sunday, July 10.

Jo was up very early taking photos while I packed up camp. Last night was the warmest so far, and tonight is the same. It's almost 8 p.m., the sun went down not long ago, and we are still in our shirts.

This morning after packing we went driving further around the Olgas, stopped at Katatjuta lookout while I went for a two hour hike up the mountain to view the valley which the domes encircle. Jo claimed he'd already walked to a different vantage point this morning while he was out taking photos. I got the impression one walk was enough.

Anyway, I set off on what seemed to be a proving ground for mountain climbers before they tackle Everest, despite the presence along the route of so-called markers. A marker I think is a small red stone thrown amongst the few million ahead to test your powers of observation.

It was a really steep rocky climb and halfway up I got stuck. I was determined not to turn back since I wasn't sure if Jo was watching from below, so after 10 minutes in the same position pondering my fate I made the effort and pushed ahead.

When I finally reached the top I realized that I hadn't climbed the ridge of the mountain but had climbed up to the saddle between the two peaks. Nevertheless it was a spectacular sight, the closest thing to Paradise I could imagine, which was lucky because I was already half-dead from the climb.

On the other side of the gorge I entered a small valley which opened out into the larger Valley of the Winds. It was green and grassy between the red rocks and filled with birds, whose calls echoed down through it. On either side of me the walls of the gorge rose steep and red, casting deep shadows into the valley. Ahead in the distance were two more domes enclosing the central valley, a strange and beautiful otherworldly garden of spinifex and sand dotted with clumps of acacias. A primitive landscape of primary colours, yellow and red and green and blue. Apart from the birds there was no sound, but instead a sense of unchanging peace and stillness, of aeons compressed into minutes. I felt I was seeing the world before man was here.

I decided to sit down since I was already on my knees and after a while looked up to see a kangaroo – or euro, rather, it was hairy not furry – sitting looking at me from a few yards away. It amazes me how they can get up so high, but he gently hopped away down the steep rocky slope without faltering.

The climb down was easier, thank goodness. After I'd recovered we set off west for Docker River Mission and the West Australian border. We're camped a few miles before the settlement, planning to approach them tomorrow morning for permission to continue through the Aboriginal Reserve to Giles Meteorological Station and along the Gunbarrel Highway.

The road so far has been fairly rough but in much better condition than we expected. Lots of bull dust which makes driving a bit hazardous. From Giles on it gets much worse we're told – the Gunbarrel is a rarely used track through the Gibson Desert.

The country has been wonderful, I think my favourite so far. Mulga and desert oak, mostly, yellow grass tussocks on red dusty soil, blue and purple mountains – this time the Petermann Ranges – and white ghost gums along wide dry water-courses. The granite outcroppings are particularly beautiful, striated and lumpy. And always against the intensely blue sky. Now at night it's filled with stars, everything so clear. At sunset, coloured orange and yellow ahead and softest lilac and rose behind us. During the day, looking up through the whitened branches of dead trees, it appears a constant deep ultramarine blue.

A few weeks later, heading for Alice Springs on our return journey through the Centre, we passed through the western Macdonnell Ranges and experienced again the immense age of the central Australian landscape.

The Macdonnells today are among the most ancient mountains on earth, the bones of a much older range which towered high above a desolate primeval landscape totally devoid of vegetation and life. Slow relentless erosion over the great geological periods wore down the range, exposing its hard quartzite ridges. The softer layers of shale were cut away by the action of great rivers to form deep gorges, today the most spectacular and vivid sights within the range.

But the small group of weathered mountains at the far western end of the Macdonnells, called the Belt Range, seemed to us the oldest of all. Drained of their redness, appearing grey and dead like a heap of old bones, they slowly dissolve into the earth.

We wondered who in the Dreamtime had wandered this way, which totemic Ancestor lies buried and untended in the ancient forms, soon to be forgotten forever. I wanted to know, wanted to share the secrets of this hard beautiful land which is not my heritage but which I know as my own.

Perisher Country

37 Mount Charles (500 m), Gibson Desert, Western Australia

"*Thin blue shadows infiltrating impossible yellows and oranges.*" C.McC

38 Gunbarrel Highway, Gibson Desert, Western Australia

39 Eucalyptus, Mungkilli Pan, Western Australia

40 Ghost gum, Western Australia

41 Mungkilli Pan, Western Australia

42 Brockman Creek, Western Australia

43 Stockmen's camp at Brockman Creek

44, 45, 46 Yelma Station, Western Australia

47 The Moonlight Hall at Wiluna, Western Australia

48 Weeloona Hotel (now used for feed storage), Wiluna, Western Australia

49 An occupied house in Meekatharra, Western Australia

50 (*overleaf*) Windich Springs, along the
Canning Stock Route, Western Australia

51, 52, 53 Wells 10, 12 and 13, on the Canning Stock Route.
The Great Sandy Desert, Western Australia

54 Sand hill country after a bush fire, Great Sandy Desert, Western Australia

55 Well 16 on the Canning Stock Route, Great Sandy Desert, Western Australia

56 Killagurra Spring. The Durba Hills in the Great Sandy Desert

57 (*overleaf*) Savory Creek (salt), Lake Disappointment, Great Sandy Desert

58 Lake Disappointment at dusk

59 Lake White (salt), Great Sandy Desert

60 Lake Disappointment by moonlight

61 (*overleaf*) Dune country; overlooking Well 22 on the Canning
Stock Route, the Great Sandy Desert, Western Australia

62 (preceding page) Well 22, Canning Stock Route,
the Great Sandy Desert

63 The Gibson Desert at sunset, Western Australia

64 Spinifex grass in the Gibson Desert at dawn

65 (*overleaf*) Dovers Hills in the Gibson Desert, Western Australia

66 (*preceding page*) The Belt Range, Macdonnell Ranges, Northern Territory

67 Sand hill country, the Great Sandy Desert

3 Wilderness

Time, time and time again, when the inland wind
beats over myall from the dunes, I hear
the singing bones, their glum Victorian strain.
A ritual manliness, embracing pain
to know, to taste terrain their heirs need not draw near.

RANDOLPH STOW "The Singing Bones"

VERY FEW ANIMAL species are adapted to desert living. At 40°C cattle will die in four to five days without water, losing seven to eight per cent of body weight each day. Without water an aboriginal will die within two days during summer exposure. A white man walking in the desert sun with no water will probably die within four hours, losing one litre of sweat an hour, straight from the blood. Soon circulatory shock sets in and death follows.

The vast distances, lack of water and scorching summer heat of the desert regions, where the temperature can rise above 50°C, frustrated many early attempts at exploration. As late as 1870 Western Australia still contained immense areas of unexplored territory, with 1200 miles of unknown wilderness between the Centre and the settlement of Perth on the west coast.

Of the explorers who attempted the east-west crossing in the 1870s, Ernest Giles was to us the most interesting, even though the expeditions of Major Peter Warburton and John Forrest preceded him. In 1873 Warburton crossed the Great Sandy Desert from Alice Springs to the west coast and the following year Forrest made the crossing from west to east. It was not until 1875, on his third expedition, that Giles successfully completed the crossing.

The route he took on his second attempt in 1873 was the one which our own route most closely approached, as we drove on from the remote weather station named after him, passing many features which he described in his journal. Over a century later this arid wilderness remains much as he saw it and it was easy for us to imagine his feelings as he confronted the desert ahead after each new setback. Every mechanical breakdown, every doubt about direction which we experienced, intensified our feelings about the country.

When Giles departed for the west in 1873, he had the backing of Baron Ferdinand von Mueller, the official botanist to the Victorian government, whose influence can be seen in the large number of Teutonic place-names on the map of the central west. Three men accompanied him, including Alfred Gibson, a young man who had begged for a chance to join the party. With a team of horses they left Macumba on August 3rd.

As we drove, we tried to follow the progress of their ill-fated journey from the names on the map: in the Petermann Ranges we passed a beautiful section of crumbled mountain which Giles called Ruined Rampart; to the north in the distance we could see Mt. Destruction, where they lost four horses due to lack of water; through the Rawlinson Range we looked for Circus Water, the last waterhole they discovered before their final desperate attempt "to grapple with that western desert."

From Circus Water, Giles and Gibson set out west to look for more water. As well as their mounts, they took two packhorses loaded with water and supplies. After 80 miles Giles discovered that one of the water bags had leaked and that Gibson had failed to pack enough food. Left with inadequate supplies, they were forced to unload the packhorses and turn them loose to find their way back to the camp, storing the food and kegs of water they carried. The two men then pushed further west into the desert.

Thirty miles on, Giles realized the hopelessness of continuing. They had lost more water and Gibson's horse was near death. Two miles after they turned towards the stored kegs, the horse died and they were left with one mount and no water. Giles gave Gibson the compass and sent him back on his own horse to the kegs, telling him to follow the tracks from there back to the camp east of Circus Water and return with fresh mounts.

Left with no food or water, Giles then set out on foot to cover the 30 miles of desert to the kegs. Choking with thirst, he reached the kegs about 36 hours later to find that Gibson had left him only $2\frac{1}{2}$ gallons of water and little food. Even after such an ordeal he decided to try for the camp 80 miles away, and after resting a few hours he departed, staggering under the 50lb weight of the keg and his meagre supplies.

After only 15 miles he was dismayed to find that the horses they turned loose had left the main tracks and plunged into the desert, and that the inexperienced Gibson had followed them. Gibson was never seen again and the desert in which he perished now bears his name.

Giles reached Circus Water weak from hunger and thirst. He stayed there a day, drinking feverishly, and then left for the main camp 20 miles to the east. "Just as I got clear of the bank of the creek, I heard a faint squeak, and looking about I saw, and immediately caught, a small dying wallaby, whose marsupial mother had evidently thrown it from her pouch. It only weighed about two ounces, and was scarcely furnished yet with fur. The instant I saw it, like an eagle I pounced upon it and ate it, living, raw, dying – fur, skin, bones, skull, and all. The delicious taste of that creature I shall never forget."

Tuesday, July 12.

A very trying day – one of those days when everything goes wrong. First of all, trouble with the car, so we haven't made much headway, although we're camped on the southern fringe of the Gibson Desert after passing through it on the Gunbarrel Highway.

A wild, frightening place. Red sand dunes, spinifex and some desert oak and mulga, which seem to be able to adapt to the harshest environment. An unconstrained bush extending boundlessly beyond your vision. Sometimes, where the winds are particularly destructive, the landscape appears half-dead and half-alive, littered with stark dead limbs. I can understand how easily Gibson perished in it and how terrified he must have been to be lost among those dunes. And it's so hot! I can scarcely imagine the heat in summer.

The country west of Giles – the Gibson Desert and the semi-arid country beyond it – still holds the fascination of the unknown, even in the 20th century. We felt we had joined a small select group of hardy explorers simply by passing through it, although no doubt our predecessors would have laughed at the idea, insulated and protected as we were in our modern vehicle and equipped with a two-way radio. Still, the feeling was there and we enjoyed it.

Thursday, July 14.

The track today was even worse than yesterday and I couldn't have believed it possible. We're making very poor time after another day of mishaps.

Jo spent all morning on the car. He went over everything methodically – fuel filter, fuel pump, spark plugs, changed all the fuel in the tank, and then took the carburettor apart and cleaned it. The trouble was a combination of things – dirty fuel, dust in everything else which had resulted in blockages.

Saw camels today in the scrub. We've seen their tracks and dung all over the road for the past week but today was the first time we've seen any. We drove over towards them but they moved off into the bush at a gallop and we couldn't catch up with them.

Friday, July 15.

Success! Jo completely disassembled the carburettor, laid it all out on the table with all the tools he needed, and cleaned it of oil and dust. It looked like an operating table. But the car worked perfectly all day! We made very good time through claypan and mulga country and camped just before Lake Carnegie. Stopped for a while at an old bush camp on Carnegie Station, a shady spot under some gums near a dry creek bed. Rough wooden seats under a shelter of corrugated iron, bunks nearby. Some small comfort for the drovers after a day's ride.

In 1896 gold was discovered in the arid salt lake regions 400 miles inland from the West Australian coast. Prospectors converged on the area and the settlement of Wiluna was established on a granite rise near a large clay pan bordered by thick mulga scrub. By 1898 the population of the town was just over 200, but by the late 1920s it had dwindled to fewer than fifty people due to the high cost of treating the ore.

When a new process was discovered for extracting the precious metal, the town boomed once again. A railway was laid from Meekatharra 116 miles to the east and by the late 1930s the population had increased to nearly 10,000. The four hotels flourished, the largest of them boasting the longest bar in the State and a beer garden. At night coloured lanterns illuminated the lawn, and a string orchestra played popular music.

We reached there at quarter to five in the afternoon. After all we hoped of it we couldn't have imagined the reality. It was totally unexpected – a ghost town of the mining era, left to decay completely and eventually taken over by a nearby aboriginal mission.

We wandered the wide, empty streets in the mellow late afternoon light, passing large buildings – banks, hotels, shops – built solid and substantial to outlast the brief, glorious boom that was to follow. On one side of the street a draper's, a "Pharmacy – Prescriptions Dispensed," a bakery. On the other a bank, a general store, a café with a hand-painted sign Bus Rest Rooms in a window on a street where no buses pass. Deserted shops blindly facing empty streets, paved not with the gold of our desert dreams but with broken beer bottles. A sad, depressing place.

Meekatharra, a remote outpost 500 miles from Perth, offered our last chance to stock up on supplies and petrol before we faced the greatest challenge of the trip, the Canning Stock Route through the Great Sandy Desert. At first sight a bleak town, surrounded by desolate country of that peculiar dead colour of blackened gibbers under an intense sun, it assumed a warmth as we got to know its people. Many of them had remained in the area all their lives and had rarely travelled more than 50 miles from the town.

The Canning Stock Route, the longest and loneliest stock route in Australia, was laid out in 1906 for the purpose of overlanding cattle from the stations in the Kimberleys to the markets in the south. The proposed route from Wiluna to Hall's Creek was to cover a distance of 900 miles over some of the most difficult and forbidding country in the continent.

Alfred Canning, a surveyor with the West Australian Government, was asked to survey the route. Reports from earlier explorers of the intense heat, vast areas of sand ridges and hostile natives did not deter Canning from leaving Wiluna on May 29, 1906, with a well-equipped expedition consisting of eight men, twenty-three camels and two horses. He reached Hall's Creek five months later, without loss of men or camels, having established locations for enough waterholes to supply the stock route. Many of these were native wells, discovered with the assistance, willing or otherwise, of aboriginals along the route. When he could not locate a well, Canning put down a bore and was often successful in tapping a supply of water. By the time he returned to Wiluna over a year later he had covered 2000 miles of desert, in what ranks as one of the best organized and most successful explorations in the history of Australia.

The route, however, was not yet ready for overlanding stock. In 1908 the Government appointed Canning to equip the route and during the next two years he put down 52 wells at regular intervals along it. From 1910 the Canning Stock Route was used regularly by station owners in the north to move their cattle south, but the long, slow journey through arid sandhill country was not considered worthwhile except in unusually wet years. Many of the wells were destroyed by aboriginals and the route fell into disuse during the 1950s.

Today the original stock route has almost vanished. A rough track by-passes many of the wells and some of these can only be reached after taking careful bearings and enduring hours of bumpy travel over spinifex and sand.

Tuesday, July 19.

We left camp outside Wiluna late this morning, so we're not far along the route. The delay was caused by the discovery that we'd camped right beside a huge nest of bull ants, and after a short discussion we moved camp in a hurry. They are so aggressive and were crawling over everything, into all our bags and cartons which we had out on the ground.

The following day we were back in the Gibson Desert. Travelling had become very slow and we were in first or second gear all the time. Until we turned off the Canning Stock Route ten days later, all our efforts went into covering the distance, getting from one sand dune to the next without too much damage to the vehicle.

Our main problem was sand bogs. As we drove further north into the Great Sandy Desert, the dunes became long high parallel ridges of sand, impossible to negotiate in places. Here they were less defined, not so high, averaging about 40 feet, but offering a deceptively gentle rise of deep soft sand which covered the wheels in seconds. We got bogged three or four times each day and had to work hard to free the vehicle.

I wondered about the drovers who used this route, who would have been on it for the better part of a year, enduring extreme heat and isolation. There is a certain thrill in abstention and denial, in the hardship of a chosen way of life: the sweetness of the rewards, like a silent sky of stars, the sense of enormous achievement at the end of months, the enriched dreams of home. I felt we were experiencing a little of this in our own way, and I could understand their choice. Back there in the desert there is always the seductive isolation and emptiness to be enjoyed after the satiety of civilization.

And then there was Killagurra. South of Lake Disappointment, in a crevice in a range of low red hills, was Canning's Well 17, Killagurra Spring. We were at Killagurra three days. From the plateau in the hills we had seen with great excitement the long white stretch of Lake Disappointment shimmering on the horizon, surrounded by dunes. Our first sight of it close up, as we topped a sand dune several days later, was spectacular – a vast area of pure white salt, gleaming under the sun.

We set up camp under some desert oak and prepared to drive out onto the body of the lake, even unloading the car in order to lighten the pressure on the hard white surface We had been warned about the deceptive nature of this surface – a thin dry crust of salt covering a soft bed of mud – and we planned to take no risks. So as soon as we felt the surface give a little not far out, we took off for the edge as fast as we could, and spent the rest of the afternoon exploring its borders. That night we saw the lake by moonlight, an otherworld landscape of luminous salt, a pale blue parody of water, dry and lifeless.

The next day we left the Canning Stock Route and headed east. At Well 24, built on a creek course amongst tea-trees, we drew some water to last us to Alice Springs. It was brown and brackish but fairly clear, and certainly essential considering our slow progress and the remoteness of the road ahead.

Despite its infrequent use, however, the road improved dramatically and we made good time, although trouble with the car later delayed us. The broken spring we suffered forced us to drive more carefully. We had entered stony plains, baked and burnt. Long days of blackened gibbers.

The flies were becoming unbearable and we were constantly brushing them off our lips and eyes where they clung tenaciously. By Sunday we were almost out of food, except for rice and packaged soup, and were not looking forward to our next meal if we failed to reach Alice Springs the following night. Memories of the desert were fast receding in our discomfort and weariness. The distant dunes already belonged to the past; ahead of us was the return journey.

Birdsville Track

68 Stockmen at Manners Creek Station, Northern Territory

69 Pub, post office and animal orphanage, Bedourie,
Channel Country, Queensland

70 Exterior of pub at Bedourie

71 Homestead at Cacoory Station, Channel Country, Queensland

72 Cordillo Downs Station, Sturt's Stony Desert, South Australia

73 Ruined homestead, Sturt's Stony Desert

75 Shearing shed at Cordillo Down Station, Sturt's Stony Desert

74 (preceding page) Dunes and spinifex; Cordillo Downs
Station, Sturt's Stony Desert, South Australia

76 Sturt's Stony Desert

"*A deep red dune contoured against a cobalt sky.*" C.McC

77 (overleaf) A wisp of shrubs in Sturt's Stony Desert

78, 79 Mount Lyndhurst Station, South Australia

80 Deserted house near Blinman, Flinders Ranges, South Australia

81 (*overleaf*) Dean Bore Creek, near Lake Blanche, at dawn. South Australia

82 Homestead near Blinman, Flinders Ranges, South Australia

4 The Way Back

For the country I travelled through was not your kind of country;
and when I grew I lost the sound of your stories
and heard only at night in my dreams the sound of dogs
and cattle and galloping horses.

JUDITH WRIGHT "Unknown Water"

MUCH OF THE AUSTRALIAN outback remains unsettled and remote because of the extreme unreliability of the seasons. Country which has been drought-stricken for three or four years is suddenly flooded the following season. Land which was parched and dry is inundated with water, roads become rivers and station homesteads small, desperate islands in a shallow inland sea.

Such is the Channel Country of south-west Queensland. We were heading south-east from the Northern Territory border for the small remote town of Birdsville, the only town in this vast low-lying area of blacksoil plains. Etched by a network of streams and channels, the Channel Country becomes inaccessible in a wet season. Its character changes dramatically with its flow of water, from a sluggish trickle in bad seasons to the volume of water which in good seasons forms three great watercourses, the Georgina and Diamantina Rivers and Cooper Creek. Between them these watercourses drain a large part of the interior of Queensland and a part of the Northern Territory.

I remembered an old man from my childhood, a drover from far western Queensland, who talked of the past and filled my head with the sights and sounds and smells of the old outback, so that I travelled through his country full of expectation. But it was no longer his country, and his tales of bullock teams and drovers belonged to the old days. I remembered his collection of bullock bells and listened in vain for the mournful mellow sound of the famed Condamine Bell in the night air.

His unmechanized outback of "a month in the saddle" spent "bringing cattle over" from the Condamine has gone. The background is little changed but men moving through it leave different tracks. Trucks and four-wheel-drive vehicles have replaced bullock teams and horses, and managers run the large stations with a staff of only a few men and a battery of machines. Mounted stockmen are still to be seen behind mobs of sheep and cattle, but the sight is no longer a common one.

Uncommon enough to want to prolong; so when we met up with a group of three stockmen on Manners Creek Station towards the Queensland border we were glad to boil a billy with them and talk for a while. The head stockman talked about the season just passed. He pointed to Cockroach nearby – "... a fair amount of water in it now but it gets higher than that in a really good season. It's dried up a bit lately. Not much rain about."

The country across the border was heavily pitted, the clay-coloured soil encrusted with a dry layer imprinted with the evidence of the last flood. Most of the Georgina channels had water in them and supported a wide variety of bird life. The few hills we saw were bare of vegetation and the pale clay colour of the soil contrasted in our minds with the red sand of the Northern Territory. Although we enjoyed the country we missed the rich colours of the desert.

Saturday, August 6.

Arrived in Birdsville today at dusk after a blowout along the road. It ruined the tyre and Jo had to repair another one to replace it. The torn tyre proved difficult to remove from the rim and it took three hours to fix. Jo broke a tyre lever and then lost a nut from the wheel so he was in a bad mood.

Camped last night in a beautiful position, in a hollow protected from the wind on the banks of the Marduroo Waterhole. We were up early after a cold night and drove on to Bedourie, smaller than Boulia, another apparently deserted town. There was no one in the "Royal Hotel & Post Office, Bedourie" so we walked around to the back paddock and saw a woman milking a herd of goats.

Jean Smith owned the pub and raised goats on the side. We liked her and stayed talking with her for some time. Two kids had been born to the goats during the night and the crows had pecked one of them to death. The other one was still barely alive and had to be killed by a young boy, the son of the shire clerk, who had joined us. He took on the responsibility for it quite naturally and I envied the calm acceptance of death which his bush upbringing had given him. Out here they seem to live closer to the bone, closer to death, than we do in the city.

The country along the last stretch into Birdsville was unexpectedly varied and beautiful – the Diamantina River lined with coolibahs, flat gibber plains, undulating low hills with a good cover of vegetation after the rains. The sun was setting as we drove into the town and its slanting rays and mellow light softened the starkness of the small cluster of buildings. We pulled up outside the Birdsville Hotel, famed for being the most remote pub in Australia, and went into the small bar for a drink. It was the first pub we'd been in which was integrated, where blacks and whites were drinking together. Birdsville felt good.

We camped on the Diamantina River just outside the town in a picturesque spot near some old stockyards. Burke and Wills had passed this way on Christmas Day over a century ago, had camped on the Diamantina on their way north. I imagined the group of men and camels under the trees, celebrating Christmas in the shimmering summer heat of an alien environment.

Next morning the vision became a reality. We had driven into Birdsville again to get petrol and water before heading for the Simpson Desert, and had heard in town about a "camel man" conducting a party of men and camels along the route taken by Burke and Wills. They were camped nearby so we decided to visit their campsite on the way. It was an impressive sight. Six or seven camels were grazing in a bed of the creek and some men were working around a smouldering campfire. We sat down to a cup of billy tea with the leader of the party and were told the reason for the expedition. Tom Bergin, a zoologist from Sydney, was attempting to reconstruct the explorers' journey in order to determine why they died. His account of the trip would form the basis of a postgraduate thesis he planned to do on the Burke and Wills expedition.

Tom's theory was that Burke, for all his volatility, was much maligned and in fact had been a capable leader forced to make difficult and unpopular decisions. Although Jo and I weren't so enthusiastic about Burke's leadership qualities, we found Tom's ideas most interesting, and we were sorry to hear later in the year that his expedition had run into difficulties and had had to be abandoned at the Gulf. We wondered if the experience had reinforced his views or altered them.

From Birdsville we took a track west into the dunes of the Simpson Desert. The most inhospitable desert of all, the Simpson has long been regarded with awe by both white and black Australians. Aboriginals feared to enter it and looked upon it as a place of death. It holds no permanent water and the infrequent rains which fall on it quickly evaporate or disappear into the sand. We had no intention of trying to cross it but we hoped at least to see the red dunes from a vantage point on the fringe of the desert and to feel the impact of the long, still waves of sand.

The first white man to see it was Sturt in 1845 and his description of "salty spinifex and sand ridges driving for hundreds of miles in parallel lines like the waves of the sea into the very heart of the interior as if they would never end" holds true today. It is a magnificent, terrible desert of 56,000 square miles, grooved by a thousand parallel ridges of compacted sand which rise like red weals on a scorched area of earth. Only the live sand on the crest of the dunes is stirred by the prevailing south-easterly wind; the red ridges of the central desert are fixed and immutable, running north-north-east in long, straight lines about a quarter of a mile apart.

Our drive was worthwhile. The borders of the desert are clearly defined and the dunes rose up suddenly ahead of us. Most crossings of the Simpson are made from west to east, since the dunes are steeper on the north-east side.

We were approaching them from the north-east so we could only manage to cross two before we had to give up. But our hopes of a view across the desert were fulfilled. From the crest of the second dune we were able to enjoy the sight of the Simpson filling the landscape to the horizon.

The average height of the dunes is 50 feet, although the highest rise to over 100. Between them lie bare gibber plains and occasional claypans. There was some growth on them now because of the recent rains, so the red starkness was relieved by pale greens and yellows. Spinifex is the dominant plant both in the valleys and on the dunes, and is so thick in places that any move which avoids contact with the sharp needles is impossible. This was not the ephemeral landscape of most deserts but a landscape for all time, permanent and unchanging. Standing on the crest of the dune, hearing only the whining of the wind down the flats, we felt that it was the wildest and most forbidding place we'd seen.

One more desert remained on our journey, the harsh wasteland of gibber country lying between the Cooper and the Diamantina which Sturt called the Stony Desert. This "iron region" of flint-like stones, which cut the hooves of his horses almost to the quick, filled the horizon, herbless and treeless. The bitter disappointment and disillusion Sturt must have suffered on facing these gleaming gibbers instead of the inland sea he had hoped to find can be read in his journal: ". . . not a feature broke the dead level, the gloomy purple hue . . ."

There are no particular geographical boundaries to Sturt's Stony Desert. He had named only a part of the vast area of similar gibber plains that make up a big proportion of the Lake Eyre Basin. We had been driving over the desert for some time, mesmerized by the bleak monotony of blackened gibbers, before we realized we were crossing it. Much is surprising about the Stony Desert. After a good season it provides unlikely grazing lands for cattle from the large stations which occupy the area, although after a season of drought only lizards and snakes can survive there. Now, after four successive seasons of rain, it produced a good covering of fodder, a mock garden through which the gibbers showed as a stark, darkly shining background to the pale green and yellow grass. In the distance we could see the luminous red glow of the dunes, incredibly vivid on the horizon. A marvellous sight.

Scattered over the stony plains are the ruins of several early homesteads founded by pioneers early in the century and abandoned by their heirs. Built upon dreams of fertile lands, they crumble and dissolve into the desert. At Cadelga the wind etches into an old stone homestead, outbuildings, a meat store. The roof is gone, the rooms gape at the sky. The sun, unhindered, burns into everything. And this was August, mid-winter in the southern states. How could the settlers have endured a summer here? Sturt, battling his way with horses across the area in 1845, recorded a temperature of 157°F. "Our hair, as well as the wool on our sheep, ceased to grow," he wrote, "and our nails had become brittle as glass."

Not all the homesteads on the plains are in ruins. As we approached Cordillo Downs on the eastern fringe of the desert, past mobs of well-fed cattle, we realized that unlike many properties this was a successful, working cattle station. The manager, John Perry, gave us the history of the place. Now owned by a pastoral company, Cordillo Downs was once Australia's largest sheep station, with shearing sheds holding 120 stands, and was one of the most isolated sheep properties in the world. The wool clip had to be carried 600 kilometers by camel train to the railhead at Farina, and all supplies for the station were brought here the same way. The distinctive woolshed and homestead were built of local sandstone in 1889 and roofed with corrugated iron, curved and riveted on the property after the four-foot sheets were carted here by camel. The massive buttresses supporting the thick walls of the woolshed are slowly crumbling but the building retains its fine proportions and solid structure. The cavernous interior now contains only old, rusting relics of the wool days which I studied with interest. The property was closed in 1937 following a disastrous drought and reopened in 1944 as a cattle station. It has run cattle ever since.

At last we reached Cooper Creek, that beautiful, ephemeral watercourse of the outback. After the rains it was wide where we met it and its banks were green and grassy, lined with coolibahs and river gums. It was such a contrast after crossing the gibber plains that we thrilled to the sight of it, the flowing water, tall trees, hundreds of screeching birds. A place of movement after miles of stillness.

We stopped briefly at the small settlement of Innamincka, an abandoned township revived by the recent establishment of a new trading post and hotel. After a drink in the pub we headed for the site of the depot which Burke and Wills established on the Cooper before they tackled the journey to the Gulf. It was here that Brahe and his party had waited for four long months for their leader's return before departing for Menindee, only hours before Burke, Wills and King staggered into the camp that same night, half-dead from starvation. Instead of their expected saviours the three men found a message carved into the trunk of a large coolibah tree, indicating a buried cache of supplies:

DIG

3 FT. N.W.

APR. 21 1861

It was too late to save them.

The scene that night on Cooper's Creek has become a legend in Australian history. Many artists have depicted the group of three men, weary with despair, confronting a deserted camp and the "DIG" tree. About a week before Wills wrote in his journal: "It is a great consolation, at least, in this position of ours, to know that we have done all we could, and that our deaths will rather be the result of the mismanagement of others than any rash acts of our own. Had we come to grief elsewhere we could only have blamed ourselves; but here we are, returned to Cooper's Creek, where we had every reason to look for provisions and clothing; and yet we have to die of starvation, in spite of the explicit instructions given by Mr Burke, that the depot party should await our return . . ."

The site they chose for Depot LXV was a paradise. Teeming with birdlife, the waters of the creek curve around banks shaded by fine coolibah trees. We remained a day there, most of which I spent watching and identifying the birds. Nearby, on a sandbank in the creek, pelicans had established a colony. At dusk as the birds come in, the air is filled with the shrill screeching of huge flocks of galahs and corellas. Graceful waterbirds perch in overhead branches or skim the water – ibis, white-faced herons, spoonbills, egrets, water hens. Kites and hawks, ever-watchful, observe the scene.

Yet it was near here, in such a setting, that Burke and Wills died. The original message carved on the coolibah tree has gone, to be replaced by a plaque. Further down the creek is Burke's grave, marked by a small memorial cairn at the tree under which he died. Nothing is left of Depot LXV. I remembered the famous painting by Sir John Longstaff, known to most Australian children, of "The Arrival of Burke, Wills and King at the Deserted Camp at Cooper's Creek, Sunday evening. 21 April 1861." By such means are legends made.

Wednesday, August 10.

Camped tonight in Parachilna Gorge in the Flinders Ranges. These are beautiful mountains. You'd really need to spend weeks hiking over them to appreciate them fully.

Our second day on the Strzelecki Track from Innamincka. Very flat country through large stations. Jo photographed an old slate stockyard and some sheds at Mount Lyndhurst Station in the northern foothills of the Flinders Range. Lyndhurst was a small town, dusty and windswept. We headed north on a detour to see Farina, the historic old town which served as a depot for the camel trains bringing the wool clip in from the sheep stations to the north. Once a busy railhead, the town lies in ruins. We experienced again the strange sensation of walking down empty streets, wandering through deserted buildings, intruding on the past. Before we began this trip I had no idea that so many ghost towns existed in the outback.

The country south of Lyndhurst before the turnoff into the Flinders Ranges is a mining landscape, bleak and windy. We were glad to reach Beltana, a deserted town which is being restored by the Hull family. The first camel-breeding station was established here in 1866 by Sir Thomas Elder, who imported 122 camels from India for inland transport and exploration. It was Elder who supplied Giles with camels for his expedition to the west coast in 1875.

The beauty of the Flinders Ranges took our breath away. As we entered deeper into the gorges and valleys, the cliffs around us became more spectacular. I understood why this area attracts bushwalkers and artists from all over Australia. The rich colours and rugged natural beauty of the hills and mountains cast a permanent spell.

Extending northwards into the arid interior, the Flinders Ranges rise as massive, upturned beds of resistant sandstone, their crumpled, broken and distorted edges forming ridges and peaks of naked rock. The vegetation varies from sparse shrubland to natural parks of native pine. Majestic river red gums grow from stony creekbeds which rarely know the rush of water except in times of flood. The area has a low rainfall and is subject to drought, the onslaught of which destroyed the hopes of many early settlers and drove them south to seek greener pastures. Many of the homesteads in the ranges are deserted and in ruins. Fascinating to look at, the mountains discourage settlement.

A hot wind was blowing as we made camp in Parachilna Gorge and it continued through the night, blowing dust and twigs all over our campsite. As it changed direction, billows of smoke from the campfire choked us and we found it difficult to sleep in comfort. But despite a restless night we looked forward next morning to exploring the best-known feature of the Flinders Ranges, Wilpena Pound.

A huge natural amphitheatre surrounded by towering peaks, Wilpena Pound was named by the pastoral pioneers for its resemblance to a pound, an enclosure used for confining stock. This oval-shaped mountain basin has a circumference of 22 miles and is drained by a creek which cuts a mile-long gorge through its side, the only entrance to the valley within. According to aboriginal legend, the walls of the pound are the bodies of two giant serpents, their heads meeting at the gorge, whose death throes shaped the encircling mountains.

We walked some distance into the Pound, struck by the rich colours of the rock formations and the spectacle of the high ragged peaks. Wilpena Pound and other parts of the Flinders Ranges are now national parks, where their unique natural beauty is preserved and protected.

We wished we could have stayed for weeks in this particular wilderness, but the pressure of time was forcing us on. Once through the mountains we felt the nearness of civilization. We were sadly aware that the Flinders Ranges had been the last area of wilderness we would visit on our journey, and our feelings as we left there were ambivalent. The thought of civilization both repelled and attracted us: the claustrophobic closeness to be endured at the end of the trip conflicted with the enjoyment of friends and of interests suppressed for months. We had been cut off so completely and for so long that we were surprised and slightly guilty on remembering unfinished projects awaiting us back in Melbourne. We had enjoyed our self-assumed role as survivors in the wilderness: it was time now to come home.

Saturday, August 13.

I can't believe we're nearly home. Two and a half months of sleeping outdoors, nights spent shivering with cold, days of enervating heat. Has it really been that long since we left Melbourne? Already we both feel more tense, ready to take on the burden of civilization.

I understand my country so much more now. I love its people, my people. Urban and outback Australia are two different worlds but I feel now that I belong to both. I hope Jo feels the same way. The land back there is so much a part of me that I feel it in my bones, coursing through my veins, giving me a love of brilliant sunlight and primary colours.

Back there in the wilderness it was also good to be home.

I would like to add a postscript to this account of our journey. The country we passed through is in danger, its wildlife is threatened and its people dispossessed of their land. Already many of Australia's unique bird and animal species are extinct or endangered. The settlers of the past were not aware that by clearing vast areas of land for grazing they were destroying the delicate ecological balance of their environment, condemning whole communities of native birds and animals to extinction.

Last century a race of people, the Tasmanian aboriginals, was annihilated. Many tribes were wiped out. This century the traditional way of life of aboriginal Australians is often disregarded or ignored. It is inevitable that many tribal customs should disappear, but the rich culture of the aboriginals should be a living one and not confined to museums. This can only be achieved on their own land.